A Critical Study Gui
AS and A Level English La
Paris Anthology

By M. Parks M.Litt.

Olympia Harbour Inc.

Tinfish Type - Librarie du Levant 2020 – Marlinspike 18190

Third Edition

Olympia Harbour Publications Inc.
Marlinspike Building, Marlinspike Place, Greenwich Conn.

A Critical Study Guide for the AQA Paris Anthology

If you are lucky enough to have lived in Paris as a young man, then wherever you go for the rest of your life, it stays with you, for Paris is a moveable feast - Ernest Hemingway

Contents

Part One – Critical Guide	Page
Stories are Waiting in Paris	4
Mile by Mile London to Paris	6
Neither Here Nor There	7
The Most Beautiful Walk in the World	9
Paris City Guide	10
Personal Narrative: Anna	11
Personal Narrative: Zara	12
Breathless: An American Girl in Paris	13
Around the World in 80 Dates	15
Trip Advisor	16
Visiting Paris	17
Walking Tour of the Louvre	18
French Milk	20
Understanding Chic	21
Memories of Places in Paris	22
Encore Une Fois	24
18 Months Later…	26
Ten Things My Kids…	27
Travelling to Paris with a Grandchild	28
Paris for Children – Rough Guide	30
Introduction, Not-For-Parents	32
Dem Bones	34
Cruise the Carousels	35
On Paris	37
Foreign Correspondent	39
Paris Riots 1968	42
Seven Ages of Paris	45

Letters from France 1790-1796	47
Paris: Fine French Food	52
Sweet Life in Paris	53
Eating in Paris	56
Part Two	
Paris Timeline	58
Examinations	62
Research Topics	65
Part Three	
Glossary	66
Further Reading	74

This critical study guide is designed to support a student's understanding of the AQA's AS and A Level English Language and Literature Paris Anthology. Elements such as mode, purpose and audience are clearly identified, and the use of language, literary and linguistic techniques, as well as tone and narrative voice, are all suitably analysed within each summary. The guide also includes appropriate exam information, suggests relevant approaches and contains a suitable timeline for Paris. A comprehensive glossary at the end gives the reader a clear appreciation of the key terms required at this level.

PART ONE – CRITICAL GUIDE

Stories are Waiting in Paris p11

Mode: video advertisement for Eurostar that appeared on the company's official YouTube channel; multi-modal, scripted with images to enhance its persuasive message.

Purpose: to persuade/advertise; conversational, familiar tone which raises idea of creating stories, repeated use of second person, 'You', engages the viewer; audience positioned as male – we see things from a man's point of view.

Audience: primarily the viewers who visit the YouTube channel and are thinking about using Eurostar and/or visiting Paris.

Summary: Paris is presented, by the male narrator with a strong French accent (giving it an authority/authenticity), as a place of possibilities; a city of romance. There are numerous uses of spatial deixis (here, there) and the language emphasises the possibilities, with several dynamic verbs suggesting Paris is a place where things happen. There are short, simple declarative utterances, and the repetition of the adverb 'maybe' implies limitless possibilities in Paris which entices the viewer/reader as they feel they have lots of choice. Neighbouring use of prepositions of movement, 'up' and 'down' add to the dynamic feel.

    The advert appeals to the senses with use of verbs such as 'hear' and 'eat' and also incorporates humour with carefully selected images. As it unfolds the viewer is made to engage and speculate on the stories implied by the rapid succession of intriguing clips. Some (the marriage and pregnancy) are linked sequentially, while others (like the catacomb skulls) appear as random snapshots. With the maybe/maybe not dynamic of the marriage and pregnancy the viewer is invited to engage with a range of narratives that are not yet written. In place of one fixed story that promotes Eurostar, our imagination is stimulated and it's difficult not to identify with the male gaze and expand the storyline. Therefore, the use of the verbal and visual message of 'Stories are waiting' appeals to the viewer inclined to create a new narrative for their own life and also emphasises the choices to be made. The simple declarative 'Stories are waiting' also makes the stories sound eager and welcoming by personifying them. The final tagline 'When in Paris' references St Augustine's saying 'when in Rome do as the Romans do', and therefore implies Parisians experience all of the activities in the video.

The transcript itself contains the generic features you would expect within a printed version of material presented orally. There are micro and timed pauses, and references to other sounds – such as the onomatopoeic 'whooshing' –are recorded in parentheses. References to background noises, the 'dog barks' and the 'parrot squawks' are in the present tense and, without a determiner (such as 'the or 'and'), can be described as elliptical; again a convention within transcripts where information is often clipped in order to be concise.

Mile by Mile London to Paris p12

Mode: book extract, written/multi modal, carefully researched. As the book cover states: 'mapped for the interested traveller'.

Purpose: to inform/ describe, focus on historical aspect. Third person narrator gives a clear description of the history of the Gare du Nord.

Audience: educated adults, as the vocabulary is relatively sophisticated, with a keen interest in train travel between London and Paris.

Summary: The use of the pre-modifier 'ultimate' functions in two ways: as a final destination and as a superlative, emphasising the city's appeal (which is underlined with the use of the second pre-modifier: 'beautiful'). Use of syndetic 'tourist, businessman or lover' reflects the city's appeal; the use of the gender-loaded 'businessman' again reflects a male perspective. Dates used repeatedly give authority and identify how the station has evolved over the years. The use of the present tense 'is all around us' and present progressive 'travelling' create the sense of being on the journey. Complex declarative sentences engage an adult audience. The adverb 'However' is used as a discourse marker at the start of paragraphs. 'New' is a key pre-modifier as it celebrates the introduction of the high-speed line, reflecting the author's own engagement with the topic. Personification, 'seems to swallow up with apparent ease', is used to make the station seem monstrous in size. Sketches are used and the maps are labelled with a font that resembles handwriting, as if the maps were hand-drawn by an enthusiastic train traveller. There is also the use of ornate typography to connote a sense of prestige and sophistication to the places described on the map. The information boxes describe the traveller's journey to the station, incorporate figurative language, 'heart of the city', and give cultural references which will be appreciated by an older generation or fans of French cinema.

Neither Here Nor There: Travels in Europe p16

Mode: *Neither Here Nor There: Travels in Europe* is a 1991 humorous travelogue/travel memoir by the North American author Bill Bryson. It documents the author's tour of Europe in 1990, with many flashbacks to two summer tours he made in 1972 and 1973 in his college days. Parts featuring his 1973 tour focus to a large extent on the pseudonymous 'Stephen Katz', who accompanied Bryson, and who would play a more prominent role in Bryson's later book *A Walk in the Woods*.

Purpose: to entertain, amuse, inform, describe and entertain. To reflect on his own experience of Paris in the 1970s.

Audience: adults interested in Europe or travel memoirs; those familiar with Bill Bryson's writing; those who enjoy Bryson's perspective as the critical outsider. Unlike his later books, *Neither Here Nor There* is marked by his solo observations; he does not seem to engage locals in conversation in his travels, nor is there as much detailed research about the history, flora and fauna of the places visited.

Summary: first person American male POV. Conversational style with rhetorical questions: 'is that asking for trouble or what?' and use of direct speech. Focuses on his own experiences, which is Bryson as the homodiegetic narrator and American flaneur. 'Good fellow' is a noun phrase used as a comical, stereotype for a Londoner and later on the adjectival phrase to present his subjective/stereotyped view of the French: 'remarkably shameless' is employed. Sibilance and personification 'sleeping streets' used to create a gentle tone. Further personification is included with 'Paris wakes up' and there's use of similes 'like a child's toy' to describe the Pompidou Centre, and 'like a postage stamp' to describe the Mona Lisa. The blunt metaphor 'London is a toilet' is used to make Paris seem more impressive. A great deal of the humour is created through use of hyperbole: 'my urine turned solid' and 'Niagara Falls impressions'.

Social comment is also included with reference to traffic. Colloquial language 'complete jerk' and expletives such as 'shit', and fronting conjunctions add informality. Compound modifiers are included to enhance descriptions: 'a well-dressed family'; as well as carefully chosen verbs, 'strolling'. Onomatopoeia is included with 'honking noises.' The past tense is used to present Bryson's reconstruction of earlier memories: 'The last time I went to the Louvre, in 1973 with Katz, it was swarming with visitors and impossible to see anything'. In the Louvre world-builders are included to create a physical sense of the place with 'entrance courtyard', 'barrier', 'door', 'corridors'. Modifiers present the masses of visiting crowds and reference queuing with: 'immobile', 'motionless', 'endless'. Verb choices also suggest the effort of visiting the Louvre: 'gave up', 'managed', 'hovered' and hyperbole is again employed to provide humorous description of cultural differences: '...the queue jumpers would have... had their limbs torn from their sockets'. At the Louvre the choice of nouns convey Bryson's disapproval with 'queue jumpers', 'miscreants'.

In conclusion, the straightforward cultural references, along with prepositional phrases to introduce cultural stereotypes, such as 'In New York', 'In Iowa', 'in London' support the relatively unsophisticated use of humour. Moreover, the small amount of French being used indicates a wider audience is being targeted than is the case with some of the more erudite extracts towards the end of the anthology.

The Most Beautiful Walk in the World: A Pedestrian in Paris (extract) p25

Mode: extract from book, written mode with aspects of a spoken discourse. Informal yet carefully crafted. Part memoir, part tour of the city.

Purpose: to entertain, inform and transport the reader.

Audience: aimed at those with an interest in Paris, particularly those keen on walking. References to American culture identify the book's primary market.

Summary: begins with an epigraph which acts as a preface for the first chapter. The first person, homodiegetic narrator is identified with the use of 'I' in the first sentence. There is a degree of informality with the use of fronting conjunctions. Minor declarative sentence 'The walkers.' functions as a paragraph to emphasise focus. Carefully chosen verbs, 'loiter' and 'huddling', identify tourists as lost or uncertain. Use of present tense makes it seem constant. Rue de l'Odeon is described as a place teeming with tourists and analogies are used: 'Yankee Stadium' and 'Lord's' for the benefit of the targeted reader (interestingly the author, John Baxter, is an Australian, yet the cultural references are American and English). Use of bathos with reference to a shopping list, rather than a work of literature. Use of metaphors: 'lost souls' and the city as 'a blank page'. Simple French words and phrases are incorporated and frequently explained, identifying the targeted audience as being the same as Bryson's. Parisians are presented as knowledgeable and keen to walk. Use of third person pronoun 'they' distances the writer from tourists - showing mild distain. The article includes interrogatives for comic effect and alliteration in line 25 makes the piece engaging as well as foregrounding once more the target audience. The elliptical invitation at the end of the chapter, 'Walk with me', hovers between an imperative and an interrogative.

Paris City Guide p29

Mode: transcript for Lonely Planet video travel guide which appears on their YouTube channel. Spoken mode, planned, multi-modal. Female narrator with a north-American accent.

Purpose: inform, entertain, persuade, engage.

Audience: adults interested in Paris and its history. Undemanding content and explanations identifies an audience relatively unfamiliar with the city.

Summary: direct address to audience with repeated use of the second person pronoun. Presented as a place rich in history and culture. Focus on cultural highlights and conventions such as walking alone the Seine. Use of positive pre-modifiers, such as 'iconic', 'grand' and 'mighty', and use of superlatives, 'most famous' and 'most fashionable', makes the audience more likely to visit. Knowing reference at the end which incorporates a metaphor: 'superlatives thrown at the city'. Hyperboles are used: 'Parisians live and breathe fashion'. Planned pauses '(8)' gives dramatic impact and allows viewer to think over what has been seen. Colloquial language is used, 'max your credit card' to strike a familiar tone. Alliterative phrases 'city's charms' and 'famous fixtures' gives the delivery an engaging fluency. Personification 'Paris straddles the river Seine' makes Paris seem grand and majestic. Written text across the screen along with sounds to enhance the viewer's image Paris.

Personal narrative: Anna p31

Mode: transcript, spoken mode, spontaneous.

Purpose: inform, to record and share own thoughts.

Audience: for those interested in Anna (such as her daughter, family members) and/or Paris.

Summary: first person with Anna focusing on her personal experiences and thoughts about the city. There are many fillers, such as the repeated use of 'erm', and pauses which, with its level of disfluency and the inclusion of non-lexical vocables, clearly convey to the reader that the text is spontaneous rather than crafted. Paris is presented as architecturally grand and easy to navigate through. Hedges, 'sort of', modify and soften opinion. Micropauses randomly appear, again reflecting spontaneous speech. Fronting conjunctions appear after longer pauses, such as 'but'. Some use of pre-modifiers, such as 'little cobbled', lovely', 'amazing', 'old' and 'big', reflecting a desire to be descriptive, though vocabulary tends to be unsophisticated due to the mode. Contractions appear, 'cause' (or coz depending on which transcript you have) and' don't', in keeping with speech. Use of repetition and intensifiers, 'really, really', and loanword 'voila' to conclude. Some discourse markers appear, such as 'anyway', to indicate a topic shift. The narrative has a loose structure and contrasts appear in order to give the listener a clearer idea of what it is like to live in Paris. The use of 'arrondissement' and proper nouns, such as 'Gare Du Nord' and 'Palais Royale', reflect Anna's familiarity with the city, and these give her account an authoritative tone towards the end. (NB. Only one page was published of Anna's narrative in the first edition of AQA's anthology. Two other pages are available online - search AQA Personal Narrative: Anna - and have been included in subsequent editions.)

Personal narrative: Zara p34

Mode: transcript recorded in 2013, spoken mode, spontaneous.

Purpose: inform, to record and share own thoughts.

Audience: for those interested in Zara and/or Paris.

Summary: first person to recount experience with Zara focusing on her early appreciation of the city and Parisian culture. There are many non-fluency features, such as fillers and pauses, more than in her mother's speech, which again identifies the text as spontaneous rather than crafted. Micropauses appear frequently. Some use of pre-modifiers, often monosyllabic, such as 'small' and 'great'. Frequent use of the intensifier 'very', which indicates a limited vocabulary and/or nerves when requested to speak; as you might expect from a young person, though Zara is described as Anna's adult daughter. Vocabulary again tends to be unsophisticated due to the mode. Contractions appear, 'they're' and 'don't', in keeping with speech, and contradictions /corrections: 'massive... well a small room'. There are also elliptical non-standard phrases: 'art good'. Words in bold indicate stress being placed on the lexeme, thus – through graphology - conveying a prosodic feature of speech. Mixture of present and past tense used to recall memories and childhood feelings. Use of temporal 'there was a time' and spatial deixis 'going there' Indirect speech appears to recount child's perspective of Paris: 'my parents heard me saying' Repetition of noun phrase 'small child' and verbs associated with mental processes 'guess', with the repetition of the perception verbs 'guess' and 'think' used to recall thoughts. Lexis associated with family members 'sister', 'parents' and childhood activities: 'Disneyland and rollercoasters' to recount expectations of Paris as a child. Hedges and vague language, 'kind of' and 'something', as well as self-correction and repair appear. Declaratives used to offer facts, personal opinions and feelings. Zara ends with a topic shift to sport and contrasts Paris with London.

***Breathless:* An American Girl in Paris by Nancy Miller p37**

Mode: autobiographical extract from book. Crafted memoir.

Purpose: entertain, inform. Nancy K. Miller, after graduating from Barnard College, moved to Paris to study French literature. In love with the city from films and novels, she hoped to create a new, more sophisticated identity for her twenty-year-old New York self.

Audience: educated American women or those interested in the city. References to her 'sophomore year' and 'majoring' indicate the primary audience, but it was clearly published for a wider, English speaking readership. The fancy font used for the chapter headings indicates a feminine, romantic perspective is about to be presented.

Summary: the language is sophisticated and reflects Miller's experience as a writer and academic. As you would expect in a memoir there is the repeated use of personal pronouns, 'I' and 'We', and the tone is reflective. Miller compares her American life to perceived glamorous life she might have on Paris. The use of alliteration, as with 'boring Barnard-girl', emphasises dissatisfaction. Use of collocation: 'fatal flaw' underlines sarcastic tone. Metaphorical language with 'under the spell' and 'France was my hedge against…' which indicates protection and a desire to escape her previous life. 'Dazzle with detail while omitting the truth' uses alliteration to emphasise the façade. The use of the word 'omitting' is perhaps used because of the stressed 't's (plosive sound, alveolar - pushing out air and not allowing anything to pass). Euphony is used when describing Paris to make it appear pleasant and delightful: 'had made everything French infinitely desirable'. The adverb 'infinitely' also stresses the post modifier 'desirable'. The lexemes 'Infinitely desirable' are polysyllabic and with soft consonants extend and soften the overall words. Other polysyllabic words, such as 'casuistry' (meaning the use of clever but unsound reasoning) appear and convey Miller's academic background and her expectations when it comes to her ideal reader.

'She wasn't 'all by herself' implies a wariness and fear of being alone. Her use of French words, such as 'femmes d'interieur', soften the sentences, and gives the extract authority. The loan word 'gamine' also enhances its validity. There is also a humorous element with 'majoring in virginity' which reflects the historical context and the use of the foreign expression demi-vierges (meaning half virgins; a girl or woman who behaves in a sexually provocative and permissive way without yielding her virginity). There are long complex sentences though her paragraphs are frequently concluded with concise points.

Around the World in 80 Dates p44

Mode: travel writing book about Jennifer Co tour. Cox is described by the publisher as leading travel experts.

Purpose: the purpose of the book is to entertain, transport, inform and give solace to those looking for a mate.

Audience: predominately women or those who can or wish to identify with a single 30-something woman's overseas dating adventure. Women frustrated with the London dating scene. However, the extract would appeal to fans of Jim Morrison.

Summary: Cox, with one failed marriage behind her, is determined to find herself a mate. She sets off for mainland Europe and visits numerous countries. In the extract she visits Jim Morrison's grave in Pere Lachaise. As you'd expect with a travel memoir it is a homodiegetic narrator with an informal conversational style which aims to engage the reader. There's the use of idioms, 'gone to seed', and fronting conjunctions. Pre-modifiers, such as 'sexy', 'erotic' and 'lithe' incorporate the semantic field of sexual attraction, although this theme, appropriate within such a text, is undermined with post-modifiers: 'unfaithful, self-indulgent and often cruel'. Morrison is given the metaphoric title of 'Lizard King' though this is ridiculed with 'Lard King', the monosyllabic word lard implying overweight and pasty. There is the foreign phrase *grave célèb* which needs no translation and identifies the reader, at least from the passage, as one who is not looking for a challenging read. Later there is a suitable simile, 'like a joint', given the context, and direct speech is incorporated. Compound modifiers also appear, reflecting Cox's desire to transport the reader. At the end there is a pun on the word door which, within the final line, is a reference to Morrison's band and captures her desire to re-enter the past. The title of her book, with 'Dates' instead of 'Days', employs a homophonic pun.

Trip Advisor: What do you wish someone had told you – Paris Ile de France p47

Mode: Trip Advisor post on a Paris forum message board.

Purpose: to share information and personal experience.

Audience: the primary audience is a Dutch person, but as a public forum it is to be shared with others keen to visit the city.

Summary: spontaneous unplanned writing with a clear degree of informality. The post opens with the exclamatory 'Wow' and uses the first person throughout. The second person pronoun appears in the second declarative sentence and the addressee is, as we later learn, 'from Netherlands'. There is the use of deixis with 'here' to reference virtual space of online community. Punctuation and spellings are not always secure and elliptical sentences appear, 'or get room soaking'. There is also use of compressed forms, such as 'restos' for restaurants. The acronym 'lol' (a form associated with e communication) appears three times and there's the lack of a capital letter when typing English. The use of the pre-modifier 'stinky' to describe the cheeses conveys something of the contributor's attitude, in that it's a mix of celebrating something typically French, while at the same time showing a degree of distancing. Repetition appears with 'Ignore' and the contributor is wary of strangers, making it clear that in their opinion this is something people from big cities usually know. Sense of distance is also created with the deictic 'there' when referring to Paris. There are topic shifts at the beginning of each paragraph and, while declaratives dominate, there are imperatives mixed in. Direct speech appears to make a clear contrast between waiters, but there is otherwise little attempt to describe anything in order to transport the reader. The writing therefore tends, although informal, to be rather functional and opinionated.

Visiting Paris p48

Mode: transcript of a spontaneous dialogue between two speakers.

Purpose: sharing of experiences, reflecting on Paris, finding common ground. Interaction between university students of a similar age.

Audience: those participating in the conversation. For wider study as a transcript.

Summary: turn taking is clear, as one would expect with a conversation and neither participant (male or female) dominates. Interrogatives appear in order to shape and propel the dialogue, for example, 'what like an accordion'. There is some overlapping, indicative of spontaneous speech. There are also false starts, fillers, such as 'like', 'we well we walked', micro pauses and elliptical, non-grammatical utterances. There is use of prosodic cues/intonation 'scary', 'loved' 'packed', 'sardines' for emphasis and to signal enthusiasm. The 'so packed' intensifier conveys the confined experience of being on the metro and the idiomatic 'like sardines' adds to this.

There are co-operative speech strategies such as back channeling, 'yeah yeah', and interrogatives to signal understanding and shared knowledge between speakers, both of whom are outsiders/observers of French traditions. The third person plural pronoun 'they' is used to describe the accordion players, indicating the point of view of the speakers as outsiders reveling in stereotypes. Personal opinion is conveyed through the use of the strong declarative 'It's ridiculous' the past tense verb 'loved that' adds to positive value judgement about the experience. The conversation is informal though colloquial language is limited, 'blokes' being an example. There are contractions and fore-clipped words, such as 'cause'. The language is relatively functional, lacking the creative flair in a planned speech or piece of travel journalism.

Rick Steves' Walking Tour of the Louvre p57

Mode: transcript of a podcast for a museum tour taken from Rick Steves' website. Spoken mode, planned/scripted. The use of turn-taking mimics spontaneous speech, suggesting natural interactions. The interactive audio guide is multi-modal with speech, music and accompanying maps.

Purpose: inform and guide, as well as engage and entertain. It also serves to promote Rick Steves' website.

Audience: those wanting to visit the Louvre and are perhaps familiar with Rick Steves, the American travel writer and TV personality.

Summary: the pod cast transcript employs a first person narrator with use of the second person 'you' to engage the listener. The present tenses create a sense of synchronous interaction: 'climb a set of stairs', 'now strolling down' and the deictic adverbs indicate when listeners should move on through the space: 'after', 'now'. Prepositional phrases are also included to guide the listener precisely on their journey through the space: 'at the top', 'at the far end', 'at the information desk'. As with Bill Bryson's description of the Louvre, world-builders are used to establish place and orientation: 'big glass pyramid', 'u-shaped palace', 'set of stairs', 'glass cases'. Proper nouns are used to refer to specific locations and exhibits, 'Louvre', 'Sully', 'Venus de Milo', giving the podcast an authoritative tone. There is a clear attempt to describe the visitor's surroundings and the exhibits and evaluative adjectives present the narrator's admiration of the space and as interpretations of exhibits: 'immense u-shaped', 'star-studded', 'noble', 'crude'.

    Metaphorical language is also used, such as 'beacon of civilisation' and a 'sea of worshipping tourists'. Compound and pre-modifiers are easy to spot and Steves' use of language employs a light, conversational tone. Ellipsis in the transcript is there to introduce key ideas and themes: 'room one (.) pre-classical...' and bold lettering is there for prosodic stress to emphasise key information. There are pauses to reflect nature of spoken language, along with more conscious scripted breaks giving evidence of the planned nature of the talk. Colloquial phrases appear, such as 'kick back' for relax and chosen verbs, such as 'breezing', promote the idea of an effortless and enjoyable visit. Humour is incorporated with reference to Venus de Milo and some self-deprecation when it comes to speaking French. There is use of spatial deixis with 'this' and 'these statues', as you would expect with an audio guide to a museum, along with non-diegetic music to structure/segment the guide. The transcript is mostly made of declaratives, but imperatives, in order to manoeuvre the visitor from one room to the next, appear from time to time.

French Milk p62

Mode: illustrated and photographic journal for teenagers. Part travelogue, part diary, part annotated sketch book, rather than graphic novel. Written multi-modal with direct speech in bubbles, thus following the conventions of cartoon illustrations, as well as the conventions of journal writing with its inclusion of personal experience.

Purpose: entertain, inform, reflect, share opinions.

Audience: teenagers and young adults, particularly Americans, interested in Paris.

Summary: During a college winter break, cartoonist Lucy Knisley - first-person homodiegetic narrator – embarks with her mother on a six-week adventure in Paris. They are there to celebrate Lucy's twenty-second birthday and her mother's fiftieth. Staying in a small rented apartment in the fifth arrondissement, they fill their days with visits to the market, cafe, and museums. These events are written up in the past tense and there's the repeated use of first person plural 'We'. The layout of a script is briefly adopted for one awkward conversation with her mum on page 63, with an unusual mix of lower and upper-case letters throughout. Explanations tend to be in parentheses. Narrator is self-pitying on page 67 and is inclined to criticise the queues in Paris. Adverbials of time appear within the chronological narrative, 'then' and 'now' and the adverb 'Suddenly' introduces the swift realisation at the start of a stand-alone declarative that she misses her friends. Language tends to be informal with use of the colloquial, such as 'pals' and 'tons' and the occasional contraction. Americanisms reflect the writer and main intended audience. Graphological aspects include the use of hand-drawn illustrations and a 'handwritten' typography to convey the informal and personal nature of the journal. The text's discourse structure is complemented by the use of images.

***Understanding Chic* (extract from *Paris was Ours*) p71**

Mode: *Paris Was Ours* is a collection of thirty-two memoirs, or personal essays, about the French capital and how living in the city changed the writers' lives forever. It is therefore crafted prose writing written for a specific purpose.

Purpose: reflect, inform, recall. The brief was to describe how they were seduced by Paris and how they began to see things differently.

Audience: adults interested in the city or familiar with the work of some of the writers, such as David Sedaris and Edmund White. Some understanding of French is expected, but unusual words, such as 'gifler (slap)' are explained in parenthesis.

Summary: Natasha Fraser-Cavassoni's contribution to the collection is a first-person reflection on Paris, style and French attitudes. It is written in the past tense, with the occasional shift to present, and includes direct speech. There is the use of simple and minor sentences for rhetorical effect and the author includes French words, for example, *citron pressée,* to give her account an air of authenticity. Temporal shifts occur as part of her narrative, such as 'A few hours later' and 'Ten days later'. A smattering of pre-modifiers help to transport the reader, along with the use of onomatopoeia with 'honking'. Other literary devices occur, such as the use of similes with 'tomatoes were lined up like jewels', and the metaphoric 'feline malevolence'. Modality in the piece is concerned with the difficulty of remembering experiences with the use of 'I cannot remember' and 'I do recall'. The focus on fashion is clear throughout and proper nouns linked to the semantic field frequently appear. The piece ends with the idiomatic clichés 'licking my wounds' and 'dig in my heels', the latter wittily foregrounding the theme of style.

Memories of places in Paris p76

Mode: transcripts about Isabella's memories of Le Parc Monceau and Sophia's journey into Paris. Both are told to a friend. Spoken mode.

Purpose: to reflect and share experiences and opinions.

Audience: primarily the speaker's friend but also a transcript to be studied.

Summary: Isabella's memories of Le Parc Monceau emphasise the beauty and importance of the park. She describes her visits to it during the day and at night and her monologue includes a description of other visitors. The park is described from the POV of the young female and first-person pronouns appear frequently as one would expect. There are micropauses and fillers, though the piece is relatively fluent and Isabella incorporates the senses (with the verbs 'listen', 'smell' and 'see') in order to give the listener as vivid a description as possible. Colloquial expressions surface, such 'skive off' and 'hanging out' and the tone is informal. Pre-modifiers appear, 'beautiful' and 'old' and 'elegant', and a positive lexis is noticeable when she is talking about the park. The eponymous adjective 'Hausmanian' (misspelt in the anthology) is used to describe the buildings she admires (Hausmannian relates to Georges-Eugène Haussmann, the French civic planner involved in the extravagant rebuilding of Paris in the 1860s). 'Really' also appears twice as an intensifier to underline her appreciation.

Her speech towards the end becomes non-grammatical and there is a creative use of language with the pre-modifier manicured being transferred through repetition to babies. Her monologue includes hedges, such as 'sort of' and there is a misplaced adverb, 'literally', when she uses the phrasal verb 'Storming through'. The end includes the thoughts of a visitor with a switch to the present tense and the use of spatial deixis, 'stand there'.

With Sophia's journey into Paris there is again the first-person pronoun, micropauses and fillers. The modifiers 'amazing', 'beautiful' and 'shocking' indicate the difference between the rich and poor neighbourhoods, with the adverb 'quickly' conveying the speed of the transformation. 'Quite', as a degree adverb, modifies her response to what she has seen on the train journey. Asyndetic listing is incorporated when she describes the members of a family at the end of the piece.

Encore Une Fois – Just Another American in Paris
p78

Mode: in the form of a typed and professional-looking blog from Anne, a mother of two 'kids'. The online blog recounts a family trip to Paris. Website/blog is multi-modal and could appear on mobile, laptop, tablet. Crafted writing following some of the conventions of travel writing. Informal, conversational tone.

Purpose: to entertain, inform and advise the reader. Anne went to Paris for Thanksgiving and blogs about places to go, her personal recommendations – restaurants, hotels, monuments/excursions.

Audience: those interested in Paris – likely to be adults and able to understand a little French (*encore une fois* means one more time). The text is primarily directed towards middle-aged American parents who have young children and may be looking to spend a holiday (e.g. Thanksgiving) away in Paris. It is family oriented as the blogger mentions much of what their children can do: 'a week with school holidays so my kids wouldn't fall too far behind'. The use of 'Thanksgiving' indicates American authorship and the primary audience.

Summary: this extract is written in first person and opens with the first-person pronoun 'I' to engage the reader. The opening sentence also makes use of onomatopoeia, 'wooosh', to make the opening vivid and relatable. The blogger uses mainly declaratives, though the direct address to the reader towards the end, 'So take a listen', is a short imperative. Dashes are used, such as 'a great idea -', to show that the point just made is about to be extended with additional information. Alliteration, with 'the tangy taste', emphasises something is keenly remembered and enjoyed. The idiom 'two bath flat a steal' makes the price seem criminally low and therefore a positive experience. Other idioms appear, 'Out of the blue', and the informal, conversational tone is enhanced with fronting conjunctions, for example 'And as it turned out'. The colloquial 'Splurging' also foregrounds the relaxed tone, as does the use of 'kids' and 'folks' and there's the occasional metaphor with 'all wash over me'. However, the focus and tone can change within the narrative. For example, there are shifts between more complex syntax and descriptive lexis in the first paragraph to more pragmatic considerations with the use of adjectives such as 'clean' and 'comfortable' in the second paragraph.

Concrete nouns and the inclusion of a modern lexis, with 'Fitbit' and 'iPhone', signal its contemporary relevance. Use of proper nouns, 'Seine', 'Eiffel Tower', 'Haven in Paris', provide specific, factual information for would-be travelers. Use of simple sentences, 'It was pure magic', with use of the abstract noun 'magic' illustrate the writer's reaction. Alliteration also appears with 'the din of the dinner', along with asyndetic listing within a succession of clauses, 'men in their scarves, adults on scooters, women whose hair was dyed an unnatural shade of red', and syndetic listing 'cheese, butter, eggs and ham'.

Direct speech 'Bonjour madame' is also included and variety is there to engage the reader. Temporal and spatial deictic markers: 'our last trip', 'our last night', At midnight', 'over the Seine' are used to recount past experiences. Additional devices to retain the reader's interest include pre-modifiers: 'delicious odour' with 'pure' and 'fabulous' conveying a subjective personal opinion regarding Paris. There are also tricolons, 'turkey, stuffing and sweet potatoes', and the use of a numerical intensifier, 'thousand thanks', to convey the writer's gratitude. It also includes a negated modal construction, 'couldn't have asked', to show the writer's satisfaction. At the end it incorporates a link to the sounds of Paris, which further strengthens its multi-modal credentials, and while the narrative is framed in the past tense the last sentence on page 79 incorporates verbs in the present continuous tense, with 'conversing', 'opening' and 'closing', to convey the experience of riding on the metro.

18 Months Later – Just Another American in Paris
p80

Mode: Anne's blog post account of returning to Paris after 18 months. Conventional use of graphology and informal language –shaped and crafted to suit its purpose.

Purpose: entertain, reflect, describe.

Audience: those interested in Paris – likely to be adults. The text is primarily directed towards Americans.

Summary: the same American POV is given and the tone is upbeat and celebratory having returned to their 'second home forever more'. The tenses are mixed with present and past 'The United flight...arrives at 6:30 in the morning' and 'I paid'. Evaluative pre-modifiers appear with 'Favourite haunts' and 'greatest hits' and emphasise enjoyment. There is also the use of metaphor with the analogy: 'greatest hits tour of Paris'. There are minor exclamatories: 'Ah Paris'; and a list of three (triadic) 'sights, sounds and smells' and sibilance.

The writing appeals to the senses, making the city easy to imagine, and by submerging the reader it meets its descriptive purpose. The alliterative collocation of 'big bucks' is comic and informal and makes the expense seem less daunting. The interrogative 'how soon until we can go back?' shows how desperate she is to return and how they enjoyed their time in Paris; which is personified with 'Paris showed us her best face' along with the 'sun peeking out', both conveying an appealing image. Again, there is use of temporal deixis with 'since our departure in 2011' which once more emphasises their familiarity with the city.

Ten Things My Kids Say They Will Miss About Paris – Just Another American in Paris p82

Mode: another of Anne's posts listing what her children will miss about Paris. Reflects briefly on her children's responses. Written mode with elements of spoken. It is planned and carefully crafted, despite it appearing spontaneous and relatively informal.

Purpose: inform, entertain, to function as diaries do: to act as a memory machine; capable of recording a person's recollections so that a shared or collective relationship to the past can be fixed.

Audience: American parents and/or those following her blog.

Summary: Parent's POV given in the first person. The use of possessive pronouns, 'my', and colloquial language, 'kids', are in keeping with other posts. Mainly simple declaratives with predominantly mono or disyllabic language. There are similes/clichés 'like pulling teeth'; and a humorous, rhetorical question at the end. Listing incorporates repetition and proper nouns and focuses on food and activities. The two images of typical things associated with Paris offers more context to the blog and, as there's little description in the text, it helps the audience visualise their experience.

Travelling to Paris with a Grandchild - Gransnet p83

Mode: website forum dedicated to grandparents. Extracts are taken from an exchange about travelling to Paris with a grandchild. Typical forum threads focus on information about the city and getting around. Spontaneous written mode with spoken language elements and emojis. The entries can be thought of as ephemeral in nature or significance, and this is reflected in the use of informal language, grammatical mistakes and typos. There is, as you'd expect, the consistent use of a Grandparent's POV.

Purpose: inform, review, describe, entertain. The sharing of information is the primary objective. However, the social nature of the forum also gives the participants an opportunity to forge friendships.

Audience: grandmothers are the specific audience, categorised by the fact that most / all of them have grandchildren and so are in a similar stage of life. No visible male input throughout the piece.

Summary Justine Roberts founded Gransnet in May 2011. It is a spin-off from her Mumsnet and targets silver-surfer grannies. The repartee is far from rapier-like, but there are fewer acronyms, such as the Mumsnet favourite: AIBU (Am I Being Unreasonable?).

Quick thread feedback appears and colour is used to highlight key responses to show a 'hierarchy' and make it easier to find important messages; the reality of Paris is explored through many different people's point of view. Despite these different points of view, they often tend to agree with each other. The messages posted can be viewed as ephemeral (impermanent) and consist of an informal, frequently hurried text, examples being incorrect spelling etc. There is the use of indefinite pronouns 'everyone'; use of modal verbs 'would love to'; use of dashes to add extra information; and ellipsis is used to indicate thought process.

The posts contain mostly declarative sentences with occasional foreign words of phrases, such as 'tabac', 'bon chance', 'bateau mouche'. There is colloquial language 'slog up the hill' 'thingy'; direct speech is incorporated 'did you drop that ring?'; and abbreviations '4yo' meaning four-year-old, 'wedding anniv'. Personal anecdotes appear; figurative language is frequently used, such as the idiomatic 'soak up'; minor sentences aren't uncommon, such as 'Enjoy'; and proper nouns (giving authority) surface regularly, such as 'Arc de Triomphe' and 'Sacre Coeur'. There is the use of superlatives: 'the best ice creams'; as well as similes and idiom 'like a log every night'. There is syndetic listing; and use of first person singular 'I' and first-person plural 'we'; prosodic features appear with the use of italics.

Paris for Children - The Rough Guide to Paris, p90

Mode: extract from a guide. Written mode, planned. Adult POV about things children enjoy doing; varied fun activities, ideal for tourists with children.

Purpose: explain, inform, engage.

Audience: parents, guardians, teachers.

Summary: modal verbs (can, could, may, might, must, shall, should, will, would) reflects choice, allows the audience to consider options. Asyndetic lists concisely sum up options, easy to read, parents won't have lots of time to sort through guides. Metaphor 'pull of Disneyland' shows awareness that Disneyland is the preferred option. Large photo of a carousel links to topic, and there is an awareness that children enjoy them. Syndetic listing gives lots of information in a straightforward way: 'with its street performers, lively pavement cafes and merry-go-rounds' (also triadic) 'including Paris Plage, Bastille Day, the Tour de France and the Course des Garçons de Café'. There is use of metaphor with 'museum-hopping'. Headings, subheadings, larger text, use of bold and capital letters all make the text easy to read and allow the reader to find what they're looking for. Informal language makes the text engaging and parentheses used to separate additional information, such as prices, telephone numbers, websites from the main text. Lists are also included and all of the above are generic features within a modern travel guide. Short declarative sentences give straightforward facts that are separate from the longer, more descriptive sentences (e.g. 'The park offers babysitting services in the summer').

Opening declarative sentences introduce paragraphs and firmly establish focus (e.g. 'Circuses, unlike funfairs, are taken seriously in France' and 'You will have little problem in getting hold of essentials for babies in Paris'). Humorous tone keeps the guide light-hearted and engaging for a family (e.g. 'but you'd better not let the kids know what they've missed'.

This is fitting for a Rough Guide which has a less formal style than others – hence the use of the pre-modifier Rough, which conveys informality. Positive pre-modifiers entice the reader ('dream day out' and 'dazzling acrobatic feats') Abbreviations in keeping with the informal style ('it's' and 'school hols' and 'Wed, Sat, Sun & school hols 10am till dusk').

'Introduction', NOT-FOR-PARENTS: PARIS – Everything you ever wanted to know p97

Mode: book/e-book published by Lonely Planet (travel guide) aimed at children aged 7 and above. Multi-modality with cartoons and text using different fonts and capitals to appeal to children.

Purpose: To inform young people about Paris (educational), as an introduction to the city; to entertain, inform, intrigue.

Audience: book aimed at young children and parents.

Summary: interesting and visually appealing for audience (children). Different fonts showing speech, key words and sub-headings, thereby easy to understand and follow. Colourful, simple and logical layout on the page/screen. Negatives used to establish text as different 'not a guidebook' and repetition of 'not-for-parents' establishing book as exclusively for children. Images that fit and relate to the information on the page e.g. the Firebird stature is related to the Stravinsky fountain because the composer, Stravinsky, wrote a ballet called the *Firebird Suite*, which was premiered in Paris. Additionally, the use of speech in speech bubbles also creates comedy. Web link for more information. More information about the Pompidou Centre is easily accessible via a web link at the bottom of the page for online use.

Mainly declaratives, which fit with the purpose of the text to inform the reader, but use of the colloquial imperative 'check out' indicates tone. Lexical choice is also typical of travel genre with the use of the superlative: 'most famous city'. Use of the second-person pronoun, 'you' e.g. 'this book shows you a Paris your parents probably don't even know about' and 'you'll hear'. This makes the child feel more involved and is a direct form of address and the creation of a synthetic personalisation. Adverb 'probably' empowers the child as they believe they have more knowledge than the parent, and this interests them. Contrast between the level of information and 'not for parents' title, interests the parents as they're being told they're excluded.

The extract also contains tricolons: 'service pipes, ducts and wires'; alliteration: 'fabulous fountain' and plosive alliteration 'pampered pets'; and fronting conjunctions 'And it is definitely 'Not-for-parents'. It also includes pre and post-modifiers which are thought to appeal to target audience (childlike lexis): 'cool', 'creepy'. There is a simile: 'like a body with all its veins and nerves visible on the outside'; use of proper nouns: 'Pompidou Centre'; interrogatives 'Is that a factory?'; and exclamatory sentences: 'I'm the firebird, I'm hot!'.

There is the use of the first-person singular pronoun in direct speech bubble: 'I brought order out of chaos'; and colloquial language is used again, with '*Loved to bits*', which aims to make the text more relatable for the young reader. The use of listing enables a lot of information to be included in relatively short paragraphs, and also has the effect of underlining the large number of activities to do and places to visit in the centre. The use of exclamation marks also adds to the desired aim of conveying enthusiasm to the reader about Paris (specifically The Pompidou Centre). Suggestions of exclusivity with journalistic phrase 'inside story'. Modal auxiliary verb in contractions 'you'll' (repeated) to lower formality and create a more speech-like register. And finally, the semantic field of horror: 'creepy', 'ghostly', 'bones', which again will appeal to most children.

'Dem Bones', NOT-FOR-PARENTS: PARIS – Everything you ever wanted to know, p101

Mode: travel guide, multi-modal (written text and pictures).

Purpose: inform children about the catacombs and what's in them.

Audience: children who are visiting Paris soon or have an interest in Paris.

Summary: addresses the audience in the form of instructions, and uses the second person: 'you have to go'. This use of imperatives is in keeping with certain travel guides and the way in which certain holiday destinations market themselves. The text is informative, in keeping with the genre: 'spiral staircase with 130 steps', and acts as a fact-file for children. Short, punchy, declarative paragraphs. Gives all the interesting and relevant information in single, concise paragraphs in order to keep the interest of the younger audience. The information can be unspecific, 'around 200 years ago', which implies the text is for someone who only needs to have a general understanding. Lots of informal language used: 'ain't' 'dem' creating a more humorous vibe which again identifies audience and purpose. Simple monosyllabic and disyllabic words: 'causing bad smells', in a form a child would understand.

Multimodal with the use of images and text to appeal to the younger reader. Array of colours used and comic art to make the page more appealing to the eye which would therefore attract the target audience. The cartoon art in particular stands out from the black background making the image strong and in high contrast to the page. The speech bubbles stand out further, with the jokes adding humour to a factual piece which would appeal to a less intellectual audience. The images provide most of the information giving a good sense of what to expect in the Catacombs. The visual content which outweighs the written again suggests audience and purpose.

'Cruise the Carousels', NOT-FOR-PARENTS: PARIS – Everything you ever wanted to know, p103

Mode: multimodal – text and images.

Purpose: to inform children about the history of the carousel.

Audience: children who are visiting Paris or would like to know more about specific funfair rides.

Summary: the piece is written in the third person with a background which utilises warmer and softer colours, such as pink, purple and orange, arguably those associated with luxury. Use of simple language allows the target audience to easily read it without finding it too challenging. Graphological features appear with the title, 'CRUISE THE CAROUSELS', in bold and with a fancy art-deco font. This use of graphology, along with the colours, promotes the idea of bygone decadence. The small amount of text in comparison to images suits the intended audience. The images, along with speech bubbles, engages the target audience and informs the children in a form other than through the use of formal paragraphs. The pictures depict the historical events in a more relatable fashion for a younger audience whilst still informing the reader.

Simple declarative sentences provide the reader with the information: 'Soldiers tested their accuracy in hitting a target as they spun around'. This declarative delivers the facts in an upbeat manner as the word 'spun' has positive connotations and injects the facts with life. The carousels have many 'cool mounts' emphasising the variety of rides and promoting the excitement to be had with the colloquial pre-modifier. Both texts have web links at the bottom for the child to find out more – introduced with the simple elliptical interrogative: 'want more?'. There is also syndetic listing: 'There are pigs, elephants, zebra and deer' and use of alliteration 'dinosaurs and dodos'. Compound nouns include: 'Merry-go-round' and contractions appear within speech bubbles: 'One day I'll win this race.' Imperatives appear:

'Stop!'; and there's the use of onomatopoeia: 'Puff!'. Second person possessive is used to engage the reader: 'While riding your horse'. There is also sibilance: 'spiral staircase' and 'seems to be spinning'. Dynamic verbs include 'hopped' and the modal verb 'could be' offers choice. Personification appears with 'merry-go-round was born'.

On Paris – Ernest Hemingway p105

Mode: a collection of newspaper articles written for the *Toronto Star* between 1920 and 1924 as a personal reaction to the city. Now collected in a book and thereby forming a detached memoir with an American perspective dealing with the external world.

Purpose: to entertain and inform. As a foreign correspondent Hemingway informs the readers of the various features and characteristics of Paris.

Audience: originally for readers back in Toronto, giving them a slice of Bohemian Paris. Now a collection of articles for those interested in the author and/or with an interest in Paris in the 1920s.

Summary: there is a mixture of first person, second person and third person. The delivery is direct, literary and can be likened to a strong, opinionated and, in places, informal monologue. The tone is judgemental, condescending towards those described, but also humorous. Triadic structure incorporates superlatives and metaphor: 'but the oldest scum, the thickest scum and the scummiest scum'. Information is added after dashes: '- all equally bad', '- but the Europeans swallowed him whole - except serious artists'. There are compound modifiers to aid description: 'strange-acting and strange-looking', 'Chinese-looking smock'; and multiple pre-modifiers specifically for people: 'a short, dumpy woman', 'a big, light-haired woman', 'three young men'. Syndetic listing appears: 'great Russian dancers, great Russian pianists, flutists, composers and organists'; as well as minor exclamatory sentences 'Paris.', 'So this is Paris!', 'The pig!'. Proper nouns occur: 'Canada' 'Canadian Government' 'Vienna' 'Rotonde' 'Latin Quarter'. And figurative language also enhances the scene Hemingway is describing: 'artificial stimulant of jazz music'. There are repetitions: 'Russians'/'Russia', used six times in one short paragraph (in this case emphasising the

37

many Russians in the city by overcrowding the text). The 'bird-house analogy becomes an extended metaphor: 'interior of the Rotonde gives you the same feeling that hits you as you step into the bird-house at the zoo.' And lastly, Hemingway isn't above using intensifiers: 'very public manner'.

Foreign Correspondent: Paris in the Sixties p112

Mode: book extract, memoir/autobiographical account combining reportage and anecdote. Carefully crafted and chronologically structured in keeping with the genre.

Purpose: inform, describe, reflect. There is a literary quality to the prose and therefore the author clearly wishes to transport and engage the reader. An enjoyable and engaging read should increase sales.

Audience: those interested in journalism, travel and/or Paris in the 1960s.

Summary: Lennon's jaunty and in some ways impressionistic book takes the reader back to the Sixties, with an account of his experiences as a young journalist writing for the Guardian and getting caught up in all kinds of adventures (best of all in the company of Samuel Beckett).

Some critics, however, have argued that Lennon has a good time reminiscing yet, no matter how congenial and informative the book is, there remains a question as to what, beyond anecdote and reportage, the intellectual interest might be. That is for you to decide, though I would urge you not to pass judgement until you've read it from cover to cover.

But back to the summary. Notice that the title is *Foreign Correspondent: Travels in Paris in the Sixties*, yet the first page of this extract sets his first journey to France firmly in 'the late fifties'. This helps to establish the second chapter (notice the TWO at the top of page as part of the introduction, setting up the perspective and background of the author. Likewise, in the first sentence Lennon does not name Paris but instead refers to his destination as 'outside Ireland' as the destination is made clear in the title.

The contrast between Dublin and Paris is then developed throughout the extract; the author often describes France in relation to Ireland, defining the culture of Paris as very different from his own. It is also worth noting that Peter

Lennon's writing moves between funny personal stories, vivid literary descriptions of setting, serious autobiographical reflections and historical analysis. The changes of subject are highlighted by changes of register and tone. With his Irish Catholic background religious references and metaphors frequently surface. Lennon reveals in several places that although he has left Ireland, he is not entirely able to give up the preoccupation with respectability that was part of his Catholic upbringing, even though 'I had favoured no such puritanical notion ever since I had given up going to confession a couple of years previously'.

There is also levity with the use of figurative language, such as 'A laconic benediction in ball-game Americanese on a Mona Lisa' (line 156) and 'I tossed myself into a holy water font of evangelical platitudes' (line 102-103). Other interesting metaphors include 'Tarnished by the acid of a thousand mechanical, unpromising transactions' (lines 481-482) and 'Scatter-gun tactics' (line 218) which is underlined with another example of martial lexis: 'battalions' (line 226). Lennon later metaphorically links two projects (getting to Paris, and getting a girlfriend once there): 'I was full now of a determination that I kept as secret as if it were a clandestine love affair, to get back to Paris, and to live there' (lines 257-258).

On a more analytical level there is the first person homodiegetic narrator; colloquial language: 'mooched away'; hyperbole: 'incarceration'; juxtaposition: 'recklessness and prudence'; compound modifiers: 'vomit-splashed exiles'; the use of the past tense; use of reported speech and – towards the end of the extract – direct speech; other metaphors: 'flooding in desperation' and 'drained of life'; pre-modifiers: 'deep, cool, sunlit'; dense lyrical quality in included letter; a tendency to contrast the Irish with the Parisians; use of proper nouns and foreign words: 'Latin Quarter' and 'arrondissement'. It is also important to appreciate that there is a literary quality to the non-fiction writing, which is evident with the level of description and use of speech.

Peter Lennon and Samuel Beckett

For those with an interest in contemporary theatre it is worth highlighting Lennon's work on the Irish playwright, Samuel Beckett. With a combination of wit, tact and sympathy, Lennon brings Beckett, who was then living in Paris, alive in his book. 'Ignorance prevented me from being overawed by Beckett' is his opening shot, and from then on he scarcely puts a foot wrong. We see Beckett playing billiards; learn that to Lennon's 'finicky ear', there was 'a trace of commonness in his vocabulary'; that 'his delivery of Dublin idiom ... was said casually, like a light salute to the homeland'. Lennon relates all this with a genuine lightness of touch, avoids all sentimentality and checks out with the end of the friendship. Lennon left Paris and 'time, absence and separate preoccupations eroded a friendship finally sustained only by New Year cards. Even that became irregular, and stopped.'

'Paris Riots 1968'- British Pathé p127

Mode: newsreel script/transcript/spoken text. Male narrator speaks with received pronunciation. Features of spoken language with pauses and prosodic features. Conventions and register of filmed news report.

Purpose: originally to inform people at the time about the 1968 Paris Riots.

Audience: the contemporary audience would have viewed the newsreel either at the cinema or at home. Now for historians (ideally those who understand the political context of the riots and the blitz reference).

Summary: the multi-modal piece reinforces the sense of drama with the narration switching between describing the protests and describing the actions of French politicians. The narration appears to be in the third person (until the use of 'we' at the end), which gives it an air of objectivity. The opening includes pauses and elliptical constructions for dramatic effect: 'France (.) May nineteen-sixty-eight (.) a nation of strikes (.) of violence (.)'. The transcript is supported by dramatic footage shot in the middle of the rioting. There is use of the past tense: 'the mob was incensed by the sight of riot police' and 'sanity and social responsibility were forgotten'. The use of the noun 'mob', with its strong connotations, to describe the protesters, shows subjectivity. However, the extensive use of the passive tense in this text arguably conveys a non-judgemental approach to who is responsible for the violence. In the phrase the 'Latin Quarter was rocked with violence' the declarative avoids the question of whether it was students, workers or the police causing the violence. In addition, the passive tense used in the phrase such as 'sanity and social responsibility were forgotten' suggests that they were forgotten by everyone. With such a report the semantic field of social upheaval, with 'unrest', 'dispute', 'conflict', 'trouble', is obvious and the other noun choices, with 'chaos', 'battleground', 'bloodshed', 'terror', 'shake-up' help to convey the narrator / broadcasting company's view of events.

However, though we might expect a news report to stick to the literal, figurative language is used to foreground the dramatic events. For example, the use of metaphors such as 'simmering unrest... rapidly boiled', 'unrest which had lurked beneath the surface spilled into the open' and 'chaos ruled the streets' add to the drama. In addition, personification, 'a country paralysed', is also used to express the point that France is not able to function. It comes across emphatically as it enhances the idea that the country has been brought to a standstill as well as the people.

Features of spoken language appear such as pauses, elliptical utterances and prosodic features. For example, within the transcript there is use of bold to identify the stress being put on certain words. Personification of Paris is also explored with reference to it being on 'its knees'. Collocations, seen in 'every walk of life', makes the speech easier to comprehend. The short and longer pauses create tension and emphasise the level of violence that the riots have caused. For example, 'France (.) May 1968 (.) a nation of strikes (.) of violence'. Figurative language conveys levels of anger and destruction. The music stopping '(music stops, Monsieur Pompidou speaks)' highlights his importance (he was Prime Minister of France from 1962 to 1968). The use of the three second pause gives the audience time to feel the significance of this 'it was too late' (3). 'Narrator: Red Danny was eventually escorted out of France (3) (music stops, chanting stops)'. Images are always in keeping with what is being said.

It is also worth listing other literary and linguistic devices. For example, use of interrogatives: 'could the general President of the French Republic solve his country's turmoil', which also serves as a discourse marker. 'Narrator: the Latin Quarter was rocked with a violence such as it had never known before' includes figurative language with a repeated emphasis on the level of destruction that Paris has endured. 'Paris will never forget there were four hundred casualties among the demonstrators'. Statistics support the authoritative tone and is in keeping with the genre. Personification emphasises weakness and how the whole of Paris has been affected in this way: 'A stunned France was counting its wounds'. 'Paris looked like a blitz city' is a hyperbolic comparison (in that only certain areas were destroyed), though there is the assumption the audience will be familiar with the term and context. Use of political lexis – orientated towards a reasonably informed audience: 'an indication that he [General de Gaulle] expects to win that referendum'. Figurative again expresses how violence has dominated the whole of Paris, to the point that it is buried under it: 'but still very much under the pall and tension of the unbridled violence'.

At the end the music reaches a crescendo and 'as spectators from across the channel we can only hope that reason is quickly restored.' Crescendo is typical of dramatic speech. The use of the first person plural, 'we', includes the British audience in the narrator's hope that reason will be restored.

General de Gaulle was the leader of Free France from 1940 to 1944. As President of France he survived the widespread protests by students and workers in May1968. However, he resigned in 1969 and died a year later, leaving his presidential memoirs unfinished. His memory continues to influence French politics and he has been labelled 'Le plus grand Français de tous les temps' (the greatest Frenchman of all time).

Pathé eventually stopped producing the cinema newsreel less than two years after the Paris riots, as they could no longer compete with television. The entire British Pathé archive is now available to view online for free on both the website and YouTube channel. In 2012 the archive was awarded the Footage Library of the Year Award.

Seven Ages of Paris by Alistair Horne p.130

Mode: history book. Written, planned and carefully crafted.

Purpose: educational; informative history of Paris from 1160 to 1969. To inform, explain, engage and entertain.

Audience: historians interested in Paris. Well-educated adults with some familiarity with French.

Summary: the historian presents himself as an objective, heterodiegetic narrator. In the extract he focuses first on the city's architecture between Napoleon and Haussmann and then moves on to the French railway system in the 19th century. He then gives an account of the poor, writes of health and hygiene and entertainment and ends with a brief mention of French foreign policy.

    The literary and linguistic devices employed include the following: temporal deixis: later. Proper nouns: Chapelle Expiatoire. Compound modifiers: Ill-paved. Foreign phrases: 'enrichissez-vous' (enrich yourself), 'terrain vague' (vacant lot) 'gare du chemin fer' (station of the path of iron – railway station). Metaphors: 'swept aside' and 'more hopefuls flooded in'. Syndetic listing: pickpockets and tricksters, prostitutes and beggars.' Polysyllabic lexis, 'ephemeral', 'opulent' (rather than rich) and 'apogee' (the highest point) indicates a well-educated reader.

    At the top of page 133 you have the subheading LIFE FOR THE POOR. This section includes Balzac's desire to describe the poverty in which many Parisians lived in the 1800s. Horne goes on to quote a passage from Balzac's novel *Pere Goriot* (1835) which reflects his concern for the poor. He also references the Puccini opera *La Boheme* with the mention of 'Mimis freezing in their garrets'.

    Though the narrative is presented as non-fiction it is worth noting Horne's use of fiction and the literary elements within his writing. For example, the multiple post-modifiers (or adjectives) used to describe the streets of Paris on page

135, 'squalid, malodorous and overcrowded', give, along with the use of figurative language, a vivid picture of the city in the 19th century. Having said this, there is also a conversational tone to the writing with the use of idioms, 'cheek by jowl' and 'hand in hand', and the not infrequent use of fronting conjunctions.

Alistair Horne worked as a foreign correspondent for *The Daily Telegraph* in the 1950s and was the official biographer of British Prime Minister Harold Macmillan. He has published numerous books on France, though the *Seven Ages of Paris* is one of his most ambitious. In 477 pages he covers the Middle Ages, the Paris of Louis XIV, the age of Napoleon, the Commune, the Empire days of Louis-Napoleon, WWI and De Gaulle.

Letters from France 1790-1796 p139

Mode: letter extracts from 18th century, written mode, planned direct (edited by AQA. Footnotes in the book have been omitted in the anthology). Conventions and register of 18th Century letter, though missing any familiar or intimate interplay between the writer and the addressee.

Purpose: inform, entertain, describe, share experiences.

Audience: primary – addressee of letter, secondary - historians interested in 18th century Paris.

Summary: intertextuality abounds in this first-person account, with its homodiegetic narrator. The letters follow the conventions of 18th century writing with many complex sentences and, as expected, are written in the past tense. However, the letters do not entirely fit in with genre expectations as they are very much a monologue with little interest shown in the addressee. They therefore – either due to judicious editing or by conscious intent – resemble an early example of reportage, rather than a simple correspondence. The fact that they were published within a few years indicates that Williams perhaps had an eye on a wider readership and has therefore shaped her letters accordingly.

Within the letters there are exclamatory sentences which convey writer's excitement at events: 'it is not to be described!'. There are also rhetorical questions to emphasise the writer's feelings about the extraordinary nature of events and the difficulty of expressing it: 'How am I to paint the impetuous feelings of that immense, that exulting multitude?' In the first set of letters noun choices convey the writer's positive feelings about events with the use of 'sublimity', 'magnificence', 'spectacle', 'enthusiasm'. The scene is presented as lively and busy with the crowd described with positive modifiers such as 'immense' and 'exulting'.

The people are also shown as active with the verbs 'assembled', 'kneeling', 'ran', 'took', 'removed'. Hyperbolic expressions present the crowd as deliriously happy with 'transported with joy' and 'melting into tears' and superlatives, with 'highest' and 'lowest' are employed when conveying a common sense of purpose. Both simple and multi-clause sentences often include metaphors with Helen Maria Williams asking rhetorically: 'How am I to paint...' and referencing the scene as one 'furnished... to elevate the mind of man'. Tripling is also a common feature with, for example, 'the imagination, the understanding and the heart'.

There is repetition of the proper noun Champs de Mars, to foreground its importance, and other proper nouns give the letters an authoritative tone. For example, Williams lists several places on the outskirts of Paris (St. Cloud, Meudon, Marly, Versailles); these were originally royal palaces and parks and Williams describes the old fountains and waterworks of the royal palace of Marly now (with the fall of the monarchy) fallen into disrepair. Williams uses a particularly long sentence, broken up by multiple dashes (a more disruptive punctuation mark than a comma) to describe the state of Marly. Williams also includes four lines from Shakespeare's *Measure for Measure.* She also references Alexander Pope, the poet responsible for *The Rape of the Lock*, and the novelist Laurence Sterne, author of *Tristram Shandy*. The assumption here is that the addressee - or her wider contemporary audience - will recognise the intertextual references.

There are two sets of letters, the first being *Letters Written in France, 1790* and the second being *Letters Containing a Sketch of the Politics from 1793-95*. By 1793 France was no longer ruled by the National Assembly (mentioned in the earlier letters) but by the much more radical and violent Committee of Public Safety, which became notorious for its public guillotining of suspected opponents. The introduction to the letters explains that Williams was a supporter of the Girondist party and that it was the extremists who held power at this point. You will notice a significant change in her attitude from the tone of approval found in the first two letters.

Background Information

The Fête de la Fédération and the Champ-de-Mars

The Champ-de-Mars (Field of Mars) is a large public greenspace in Paris, located in the seventh arrondissement. The park is named after the Campus Martius (Mars Field) in Rome, a tribute to the the Roman God of war. The name also alludes to the fact that the lawns here were formerly used as drilling and marching grounds by the French military.

Originally, the Champ de Mars was part of a large flat open area called Grenelle, which was reserved for market gardening. Citizens would claim small plots and exploit them by growing fruits, vegetables, and flowers for the local market. The construction in 1765 of the École Militaire was the first step toward the Champ de Mars in its present form. Jacques Charles and the Robert brothers launched the world's first hydrogen-filled balloon from the Champ-de-Mars on 27 August 1783.

This place witnessed the spectacle and pageantry of some of the most well-remembered festivals of the French Revolution. On 14 July 1790 the first 'Federation Day' celebration (Fête de la Fédération), now known as Bastille Day, was held on the Champ de Mars, exactly one year after the storming of the prison. The following year, on 17 July 1791, the massacre on the Champ de Mars took place. Jean Sylvain Bailly, the first mayor of Paris, became a victim of his own revolution and was guillotined there on 12 November 1793.

Louis XVI and Marie Antoinette

On 21 June 1791 Louis XVI was captured in Varennes, about thirty miles from the monarchist stronghold of Montmédy near the German border. The rumour was that he'd been kidnapped, but it soon became clear that, unwilling to accept constitutional limits on his power, he was on his way to join the Marquis de Bouillé and the Austrian army. This abortive escape attempt only deepened fears of foreign invasion. In the autumn, the Girondins began to advocate pre-emptive strikes against German states harbouring French nobles and priests. Before long, deputies began to feel they had a moral duty to spread freedom across national borders. 'The moment has come,' Brissot proclaimed, 'for a crusade of universal liberty.' War was declared against Austria in April 1792.

By September 1792 the atmosphere in Paris was tense. Rumours were spreading that the city's prisoners – nobility, Swiss Guards and priests – planned to escape and launch a counter-revolution. Fearful of what the prisoners might do, gangs of sans-culottes entered the jails and killed more than a thousand inmates as their jailers stood by. The violence was popular, spontaneous and vengeful.

The September massacres are generally considered to be the point at which popular violence became state-sponsored Terror. The debate on how best to bring the king to justice divided left from right: Robespierre's Montagnards wanted a swift trial and execution; the Girondins proposed a referendum to approve the Convention's decisions. Jean Debry, who eventually voted for execution, recalled how he 'agonised over the truth of the matter'. On the morning of 21 January, in front of nearly a hundred thousand people on the place de la Révolution, Louis XVI was beheaded.

Despite her attempts to remain out of the public eye, Marie Antoinette was falsely accused of conducting an affair with La Fayette, whom she loathed, and, as was published in Le Godmiché Royal (The Royal Dildo), of having a sexual relationship with Lady Sophie Farrell of Bournemouth, a well-known lesbian. Publication of such calumnies continued to the end, climaxing at her trial in October 1793 with that of incest with her son.

After her trial her hair was shorn, her hands bound painfully behind her back and she was leashed with a rope. Unlike her husband, who had been taken to his execution in a carriage (carrosse), she had to sit in an open cart (charrette) for the hour it took to reach the guillotine erected in Place de la

Révolution, (present-day Place de la Concorde). She maintained her composure, despite the insults of the jeering crowd. For her final confession, a constitutional priest was assigned to her. He sat by her in the cart, and she ignored him all the way to the scaffold.

Marie Antoinette was guillotined at 12:15 p.m. on 16 October 1793. Her last words were 'Pardon me, sir, I meant not to do it', to Henri Sanson, the executioner, whose foot she had accidentally stepped on after climbing to the scaffold. Her body was thrown into an unmarked grave in the Madeleine cemetery located close by.

Helen Maria Williams

Helen Maria Williams travelled to France in July 1790 to take part in the Fête de la Fédération that marked the first anniversary of the fall of the Bastille. She described the pageantry at the Champ de Mars as the 'triumph of humankind; it was man asserting the noblest privilege of his nature; and it required but the common feelings of humanity, to become in that moment a citizen of the world.'

In 1794, in the midst of the Terror, she felt differently:

I have no words to paint the strong feeling of reluctance with which I always returned from our walks in Paris, that den of carnage, that slaughterhouse of man … We were obliged to pass the square of the revolution, where we saw the guillotine erected, the crowd assembled for the bloody tragedy, and the gens d'armes on horseback, followed by victims who were to be sacrificed, entering the square. Such was the daily spectacle which had succeeded the painted shows, the itinerant theatres, the mountebank, the dance, the song, the shifting scenes of harmless gaiety, which used to attack the cheerful crowd as they passed from the Tuileries to the Champs Elysées.

'Paris: Fine French Food' – Lonely Planet p148

Mode: transcript from advert, spoken mode video travel guide produced by Lonely Planet for their official YouTube channel. Male narrator with an antipodean (Australian) accent.

Audience: adults who have an interest in food and Paris.

Purpose: to sell and market Paris as the food capital of the world. It is also to persuade the audience to travel to Paris. Persuade, entertain, describe, inform.

Summary: words typed in bold are emphasised by the narrator, hence a prosodic feature. Spatial deixis of 'here' is used to communicate the idea the narrator is in Paris, a city which is described as 'the culinary centre of the most gastronomic country in the world.' The use of the superlative is in keeping with the world of advertisements and intensifiers, such as 'very' add to the positive message. The video travel guide emphasises the variety of eateries, with reference to a traveller's budget, and the diversity of food available. The repeated use of the second-person pronoun, 'you', is also typical in that the advert wishes to draw the viewer in. The language and delivery is upbeat in tone and contractions appear, indicating a level of informality. The text also contains many factual pieces of information, giving it an authority and a gloss of objectivity. The text includes a little French, such as fromagerie, which is easily understood given the context.

The Sweet Life in Paris: Delicious Adventures in the World's Most Glorious and Perplexing City – **David Lebovitz p150**

Mode: book extract is about drinking water in Paris; written mode, planned. Also includes a recipe. First person (homodiegetic) narrator gives an autobiographical experience recounted retrospectively. The adult male American writer shares his interest in and knowledge of food, drink and dining out gained through his occupation as both a professional chef and writer. The extract includes genre conventions associated with travel writing

Purpose: written to inform and entertain the targeted audience about Paris and the culture. Paris is presented as unclean, reliant on water, controlled by the Seine/water purification. There is a distinct difference between the Parisian and the tourist.

Audience: aimed at an educated audience, arguably American tourists, interested in Paris and its culture (there are a number of French phrases used with no translation suggesting the author believes his readership would already know what the words/phrases mean).

Summary: the layout in the anthology is just the same as it is in the book. The double-spaced lines make the opening page of the chapter easy to read and the image relates to the semi-circular iron bars used for protecting historic buildings from men 'relieving themselves.'

The structure of the prose piece, which dominates chapter six, is straightforward with Lebovitz reflecting on the drinking water in Paris and then on the issue of 'getting rid of it'. The homodiegetic narrator is easy to spot with inclusive first-person plural pronouns 'our' and 'we'. The register is informal with its use of fronting conjunctions, such as 'Because' and 'And'. The use of contractions 'you'd think it would be easy to get a glass of the stuff' add to the informality. There are also compound modifiers, including 'hot-shot' and 'state-of-the-art'. The use of interrogatives allows the narrator to connect with the reader and again makes it less formal. There is alliteration, 'moisture in my mouth' and 'tiny trickle', which emphasises the lack of water. There is personal reflection and an admission of weakness: 'I haven't built up the courage to ask'. This again encourages the reader to sympathise with the narrator.

Simple non-grammatical sentences, such as 'I got it', vary the pace. The use of French, often without translation, suggests that the target audience is relatively well educated. This is also underlined with the polysyllabic lexis used to add descriptive details: 'parsimoniously', 'sequestered', 'dessicated', 'panopoly'; words which also reflect the literary genre and crafted written mode. Comparisons, such as 'is like going into Starbucks and saying, 'I'd like coffee' or going to a multiplex cinema and telling the cashier, 'I'd like a ticket to see a movie', allow the reader to understand the narrator by comparing the topic to subjects that the target audience can relate to.

Personal observations also appear: 'unlike my neighbour down the hall, who evidently doesn't consider showering all that important'. These also add humour as does the colloquial lexis with: 'stuff' and 'chugging'. Furthermore, there are tag questions and the direct address with the use of the second person pronoun used to convey humour: 'you don't want to ruin this for the rest of us by drinking water, do you?' Water appears quite rare and the use of nouns and verbs more commonly associated with wartime emphasise the small amount of water provided: 'ration', 'rationed. It is 'Meant to be consumed in carefully controlled, measured doses' and the lexical field of small amounts emphasises how little water the French make available: 'sip', 'tiny', 'small', 'smaller'. Moreover, adverbials suggest a negative French attitude towards the provision of water at mealtimes: 'With some reluctance, she reached down' and it is described as 'pas jolis (not beautiful)'. However, there are long lists of consecutive interrogatives and proper nouns for brands of water to reflect the many options available: 'San Pellegrino or Perrier?

Châteldon or Salvetat? Badoit or Evian?' Dashes are also used throughout to indicate that extra information will follow. In some cases this may be used to add personal information (anecdote): 'I've yet to see one anywhere – except on eBay.fr.' There is also the use of a minor exclamatory: 'Yuck!'

After reflecting on the 'daunting' amount of effort required 'to get a sip' at dinner in Paris, Lebovitz moves on to a recipe for a Mexican dish: Chocolate Mole. He links to the previous chapter in the first sentence and incorporates the hyperbole 'endless' when referencing his 'quest for water'. He uses the plural pronoun 'our' to identify with his primary audience (fellow Americans). The pre-modifier 'Authentic' is significant when identifying Mexican products and leads to the use of the colloquial verb 'lug' when importing his own ingredients. Rhetorical questions are incorporated, 'And how can you not love mole?', and the use of the fronting conjunction emphasises the informal, conversation tone. In the list of ingredients there are pre-modifiers, such as unsweetened, and verbs in the past tense, such as 'chopped', 'sliced'. The instructions consist of imperatives, as you would expect, with an elliptical element – in that unnecessary words, such as pronouns, are not included. The instructions are written in the present tense and include prepositions of time: 'until' and 'for'.

Eating in Paris p158

Mode: transcript from a conversation between friends, spoken discourse/mode, spontaneous communication. The transcript is part of a multi-speaker discourse involving three speakers talking about their memories of visiting and eating in Paris. All three are students. Mike and Sophia were born in the UK while Isabelle comes from France.

Purpose: sharing culinary experiences in Paris and reflecting on different tastes. The conversation is interactional and presents the informal relationship between university students of a similar age.

Audience: those taking part in the conversation (primary). Secondary audience are readers of the transcript.

Summary: the three-way conversation contains first person singular pronouns throughout and the past tense verbs convey memories from personal experience: 'I got it',
'it looked'. Each participant shares his or her opinions about French cuisine with Mike showing a very blinkered attitude towards traditional dishes. Comparisons are made, with snails likened twice by Mike to eating mud. Adjectives convey strong personal opinions about some French foods: 'disgusting', 'lovely' and the colloquial lexis reflects the informal context of friends talking: 'stuff', 'peckish'. Non-lexical onomatopoeia is used to convey feelings of distaste or disgust 'eugh'. Topic shifts from Isabelle mention more attractive aspects of French food and her background allows her to share a more intimate knowledge of French food and culture: 'pork', 'they're tiny little choux balls'. Juxtaposition reflects the diversity of French food and the speaker's contrasting feelings towards it: 'blood and guts', 'lovely patisseries'. The verb 'dip' is in bold to emphasise the stress Isabelle places on the action. Intensifiers appear with the use of 'very', 'really' and 'so'. There are simple pre-modifiers,

like the repeated 'nice' and the general register is unsophisticated.

However, the incorporation of French by Isabelle elevates the lexis and reflects her wider and superior cultural understanding. Lexemes from the semantic field of eating occurs frequently, for example 'bread' 'six courses' etc. Micro pauses show the text is spontaneous and overlapping reveals how the speakers are relaxed with each other as they are not strictly following formal conventions such as turn taking. There is alliteration 'best bread', though it's impossible to say whether it's intentional. Filler words 'you know', 'like' appear and repetition again demonstrates spontaneity: 'it (.) it's like'. There is also back-channelling and elliptical sentences common to spontaneous spoken discourse: 'yeah', 'like', 'basically', 'don't want that'. Furthermore, Mental verb phrases to reflect insecure knowledge: 'I think it's pork' and idiomatic spatial metaphors indicate personal opinion: 'it's not necessarily right down my alley'. The descriptions in parentheses, '(laughter)', shows that the three participants are comfortable enough to enjoy their conversation.

PART TWO - PARIS TIMELINE

250-225 BCE A Celtic tribe known as the Parisii, found Lucotecia, on the Île de la Cité.

53 BCE Julius Caesar addresses an assembly of leaders of the Gauls in Lucotecia, asking for their support.

511 Clovis I, the king of the Franks, makes Paris his capital.

1120 As Notre-Dame is not large enough to house them all, teachers and students begin to take up residence on the left bank. This is the beginning of the Latin Quarter and the Sorbonne.

1231 They begin to drain the marshes, creating Le Marais.

1470 Publication of *Letters* by Gasparin de Bergame, the first book to be printed in France.

1535 Marie la Catelle, a schoolteacher is burned at the stake for reading the *New Testament* in French to her pupils. A month later Etienne de La Forge is burned at the stake for printing the *New Testament* and distributing them to the poor.

1544 The Sorbonne publishes the first *Index*, or list of forbidden books.

1622 A windmill is built atop Montmartre. In the 19th century it becomes a famous landmark, known as the Moulin de la galette.

1641 First permanent theatre opens within the Palais-Royal.

1659 Molière performs at the Louvre.

1660 Introduction of coffee. Served in Marseille in 1626, it did not become popular in Paris until 1669.

1716 The founding of the first private bank in Paris, the Banque générale, by the Scotsman John Law. Four years later the bank collapses with rioters demanding to exchange their banknotes for silver.

1723 In an effort to improve censorship a royal regulation forbids printing houses and publishing outside of the Latin quarter on the Left Bank.

1770 Firework display to celebrate the marriage of the Dauphin and Dauphine (the future king Louis XVI and queen Marie-Antoinette) ends in tragedy with 132 killed.

1783 Treaty of Paris is signed between the United States and Britain, ending the American Revolution.

1786 The first recognisable restaurant, the Taverne anglaise, is opened in Paris. It is allowed to serve customers until eleven in the evening in winter and midnight in summer.

1788 Devastating hail storms and strong winds destroy crops and orchards, causing a major increase in bread prices. Thousands of peasants migrate to Paris. The French state becomes bankrupt and large-scale demonstrations begin.

1789 The Bastille is stormed on 4th July. Several prisoners are released. The governor, after having been promised safe passage, is lynched by the crowd. In October Louis XVI and his family are forced to leave Versailles for Paris.

1790 The Fête de la Fédération, celebrates the first anniversary of the Revolution on the 14th July.

1791 Louis XVI and his family flee Paris, but are captured and brought back.

1793 Louis XVI is executed in January on the Place de la Révolution. Marie Antoinette is executed in October. By law the French citizens are required to use the familiar personal pronoun 'tu' rather than the formal 'vous'. All churches are closed by the government.

1794 June marks the climax of Reign of Terror (Grande Terreur). Over 1,000 citizens are executed.

1799 In November Napoléon Bonaparte stages a coup d'état and dissolves the government.

1801 With Paris's population having grown to 548,000, Napoleon orders the creation of three new cemeteries outside the city: Montmartre to the north; Père-Lachaise to the east; Montparnasse to the south.

1804 In December Napoleon crowns himself Emperor at Notre Dame Cathedral.

1815 Napoleon is defeated at the Battle of Waterloo in Belgium.

1838 Louis Daguerre takes the first modern photograph of a man having his shoes shined.

1846 The population of Paris climbs above a million. The first Gare du Nord railway station is completed.

1853 Georges-Eugène Haussmann begins the demolition of medieval neighbourhoods. The appearance of the centre of Paris today is largely the result of his work.

1854 Louis Vuitton opens his luggage shop.

1859 The previous twelve arrondissements are reorganized into twenty.

1871 The Prussians bombard Paris with heavy siege guns before entering the city. The Paris council (or Commune) is dominated by anarchists, radical socialists and revolutionary candidates. The Commune is attacked by the French army.

Approximately 10,000 communards are killed and over 40,000 Parisians are put in prison.

1871 The beginning of what is referred to as La Belle Époque (conventionally dated from the end of the Franco-Prussian War to the beginning of WWI).

1889 Opening of the Eiffel Tower.

1895 First projected showing of a motion picture by Louis Lumière. Le Cordon Bleu cooking school opens.

1900 Opening of the first line of the Paris Métro.

1903 The population now stands at just below 3 million. Start of the first Tour de France.

1907 Pablo Picasso is living in Montmartre.

1910 Coco Chanel opens her first boutique, Chanel Modes.

1919 Sylvia Beach's Shakespeare and Company bookshop opens.

1921 In November Ernest Hemingway arrives as a correspondent for the *Toronto Star* with his wife Hadley. He remains in Paris until 1928.

1940 German troops enter Paris. Four years later they will surrender to the Allied forces.

1968 Student demonstrations spread to the Sorbonne. The unrest culminates in a general strike.

EXAMINATIONS

AS English Language and Literature

With the AS exam (Paper 2 – People and Places) you have 1 hour and 30 minutes to complete Sections A and B. AQA recommends that you spend about 50 minutes on Section A (comparing two extracts) and 40 minutes on Section B (re-creative and analysis of own writing). There are 40 marks for the question from Section A and a total of 35 marks for the questions from Section B. For Section B it is important to write creatively, within the given genre, and include relevant information. For your critical analysis of your own work you should keep to 4 short paragraphs, of no more than 50 words each. Each paragraph should deal with a particular aspect.

Both the AS and the A Level will require you to compare two pieces from the anthology. At AS Level the focus appears to be on how Paris is presented, with both the 2016 and 2017 papers asking students to compare and contrast how the speaker/s and/or writer/s present Paris in the two extracts.

With the A-level it might require you to reflect on a particular aspect or theme that the two pieces have in common. For example, in June 2017 A-level students were required to compare and contrast how the writer and speaker of the chosen texts expressed their ideas about times of social upheaval in Paris. In June 2018 the extracts were taken from *Neither Here Nor There: Travels in Europe* by Bill Bryson and from Rick Steves' Walking Tour of the Louvre Museum. Students were asked to compare and contrast how the writers presented experience of visiting the Louvre. In 2019 students needed to compare and contrast how the speakers of Text A and the writer of Text B expressed their ideas about food or drink in Paris.

A Level English Language and Literature

With the A level (7707) you will be required to answer on the Paris Anthology in Section A – Question 1 of Paper 1. You will be required to compare and contrast two extracts and there are three marks awarded for this question on the following assessment objectives:

>**AO1** (15 marks) – Apply concepts and methods from integrated linguistic and literary study as appropriate, using associated terminology and coherent written expression.
>
>**AO3** (15 marks) – Demonstrate understanding of the significance and influence of the contexts in which texts are produced and received.
>
>**AO4** (10 marks) – Explore connections across texts, informed by linguistic and literary concepts and methods.

Using the assessment objectives above, the examiner will assess your ability to explore connections between texts and highlight similarities and differences. However, you must focus on the task set throughout your response.

You must also show a clear understanding of the contexts, genres and modes of both texts, discuss how the language was influenced by the writers' stances and contexts of production, compare linguistic details of the texts, cover the texts equally, support ideas by exploring the language of relevant examples, apply terminology accurately, explore in detail how meanings are shaped, provide interpretations that are well supported by detailed evidence from the text and, lastly, produce a sustained and developed answer which is well expressed and clearly structured answers.

It is also advisable not to deal with one extract and then, when half way through, switch your attention to the other. It is far better to identify elements, such as mode, use of figurative language etc., and to focus on these elements within a paragraph or two and deal with each extract in turn.

RESEARCH TOPICS

The wider research topics will help you to become better informed and are ideal for class presentations. It is also worth mentioning that Woody Allen's film *Midnight in Paris* (2011) gives you a wonderful introduction to the city and its past.

The Bastille and the French Revolution 1789-99

Pigalle and Montmatre

Latin Quarter and the Sorbonne

Marias and Montparnasse

French Writers: Hugo, Balzac, Zola, Simone de Beauvoir

Parisian Newspapers

Paris in the 1920s-70s

Shakespeare and Co.

Pere Lachaise

Bohemian Paris: 1830-1930 (artists, writers, film-makers and the Parisian flâneur)

La Belle Époque (conventionally dated from the end of the Franco-Prussian War in 1871 to 1914)

Americans in Paris: Hemingway, Fitzgerald and Josephine Baker

The Louvre

Olympia Press

PART THREE – GLOSSARY

Anaphoric and Cataphoric: an anaphoric reference means a word refers back to another word for its meaning. Susan dropped the plate. It shattered loudly. Cataphoric reference means that a word in a text refers to another later in the text and you need to look forward to understand. If you want some, here's some parmesan cheese.

Aposiopesis: where a sentence is deliberately broken off and left unfinished, the ending to be supplied by the imagination, giving an impression of unwillingness or inability to continue. An example would be the threat "When I get hold of you I'll —!" This device often portrays its users as overcome with passion (fear, anger, excitement or even modesty). To signify the use of aposiopesis a dash (—) or an ellipsis (…) may be used. The most effective use of aposiopesis is when the reader can successfully figure out the missing thoughts that the writer has left unfinished.

Collocation: a sequence of words or terms that occur more often than would be expected by chance.

Compound Verbs: the English lexicon contains a few true compound verbs, such as stirfry, kickstart and forcefeed.

Conjunctions: include 'and, or, but, because, although' and join two parts of sentences. Conjunctions can be used to give more information, give alternatives, give reasons, give results or give unexpected information.

Deictic Expression: (deixis) a deictic expression is a word or phrase (such as this, that, these, those, now, then) that points to the time, place, or situation in which a speaker is speaking. In the short sentence 'You should have been here last week' *you* is an example of personal deixis, *here* is an example of spatial deixis, and *last week* is an example of temporal. Temporal deixis includes time adverbs like now, then, soon.

It is important therefore to remember that person deixis will use personal pronouns: 'I', 'you', and 'we', etc; or demonstrative pronouns 'it', 'this', 'that', etc. Spatial deixis will use locative expressions such as 'here', 'there', 'nearby' and verbs suggesting direction towards or away from the speaker ('come' and 'go'). Temporal deixis will employ temporal adverbs 'soon', 'now', and 'then' and other temporal expressions such as 'tomorrow', 'next year', 'a while ago'.

Deictic language helps to create the spaces and temporal settings of fictional and non-fictional worlds, and facilitates in determining the positioning and orientation of narrators or participants.

Epistemic: when a modal verb is used to express the speaker's opinion about a statement, then this is epistemic modality: It *might* be true. Here, the speaker is expressing their attitude about whether it is true or not, accepting that there is a possibility, but not being certain. It therefore deals with a speaker's evaluation/judgment of, degree of confidence in, or belief of the knowledge upon which a proposition is based. In other words, epistemic modality refers to the way speakers communicate their doubts, certainties, and guesses.

Free Indirect Discourse or Speech: is a third person narrative which uses some of the characteristics of third-person along with the essence of first person direct speech. What distinguishes free indirect discourse or speech from normal indirect speech is the lack of an introductory expression such as 'She said' or 'She thought'. It is as if the subordinate clause carrying the content of the indirect speech is taken out of the main clause. Using free indirect speech may convey the character's words more directly than in normal indirect, as devices such as interjections and exclamation marks can be used that cannot be normally used within a subordinate clause. Jane Austen is cited as one of the first writers to use this style consistently.

Quoted or direct speech: He laid down his heavy bundle and thoughts turned to his sickly mother. 'And just what pleasure have I found, since I came into this melancholy world?' he asked.

Reported or normal indirect speech: He laid down his heavy bundle and his thoughts turned to sickly mother. He asked himself what pleasure had he found since he came into the melancholy world.

Free indirect speech: He laid down his heavy bundle and his thoughts turned to his sickly mother. And just what pleasure had he found, since he came into this melancholy world?

Genre: a way of grouping, categorising and classifying texts based on expected shared conventions. Genres come into being as the result of people agreeing about perceived similar characteristics in terms of content or style. However, genres are fluid and dynamic and new genres continually evolve. For example, post-horror with *A Ghost Story*, in which Casey Affleck is basically a human emoji of a ghost.

Graphology: the visual elements of a text. There are various elements to it, including: layout, font sizes and type, use of images, use of colour. The layout of a text is often related to its genre. For example, shopping lists, emails, menus and advertisements all tend to have prototypical layout features so that they are visually easily recognisable.

Typographical features are those related to the way that fonts are used and set out in texts. These may include aspects of type, size, colour, effects (for example, using bold, underlined or italicised font), the choice of background against which a font is set, and any spacing that is used. The careful use of typographical features can help readers to follow writing clearly, highlight important points, and aim to produce dramatic effects. If you talk about graphology, it's important to consider why it has been used.

Implicature: an implied meaning that has to be inferred as a result of a conversational maxim being broken. The action of implying a meaning beyond the literal sense, for example saying the frame is nice and implying I don't like the picture in it. The aspect of meaning that a speaker conveys or suggests without directly expressing. Although the utterance 'Can you pass the salt?' is literally a request for info about one's ability to pass salt, the understood implicature is a request for salt.

Intensifiers: a special kind of adverb. An intensifier is used when the semantic value of another adverb or adjective needs to be altered. Examples of intensifiers are: very, quite, absolutely and extremely but there are many more. Intensifiers act to pre-modify their adverb or adjective, such as terrifically in 'It was a terrifically bad accident.'

Interdiscursivity: the use of discourses from one field as part of another (e.g. the use of science discourses in the selling of beauty products, or the use of commercial discourses in education).

Isocolon: a figure of speech in which a sentence is composed of two or more parts (cola) perfectly equivalent in structure, length and rhythm: it is called bicolon, tricolon, or tetracolon depending on whether they are two, three, or four. An example of bicolon is the advertising slogan 'buy one, get one free'. Julius Caesar's Veni, vidi, vici (I came; I saw; I conquered) is a well-known tricolon. A tricolon that comprises parts in increasing size, magnitude or intensity is called a tricolon crescens, or an ascending tricolon. A tricolon that comprises parts that decrease in size, magnitude, intensity, or word length is called a tricolon diminuens or a descending tricolon. 'I have nothing to offer but blood, toil, tears, and sweat' is Churchill's famous tetracolon.

Loanword: is a word adopted from one language (the donor language) and incorporated into another language without translation, for example café (from the French café, which literally means coffee), kindergarten (from German kindergarten, meaning children's garden) and jodhpurs from Hindi. Loans of multi-word phrases, such as the use of déjà vu, are known as lexical borrowings.

French continues to be the largest single source of new words outside of our scientific and technical vocabulary, which is still dominated by classical borrowings). Examples of French loanwords and lexical borrowings include: ballet, chaise longue, champagne, chic, clique, cognac, denim, faux pas, grotesque, nom de plume, quiche, rouge, sachet, salon, saloon.

In some cases, the original meaning shifts dramatically through unexpected leaps. The word Viking, for example, became the Japanese baikingu, meaning buffet. This is because in 1958 Imperial Viking was the first restaurant in Japan to offer buffet-style meals.

Literariness: the degree to which a text displays qualities that mean that people see it as literary and as literature. However, since many so called 'non-literary' texts display aspects of creative language use that is often seen as a marker of being literary, it is best to think of literariness as a continuum rather than viewing texts as being absolutely 'literary' or 'non-literary'.

Modal Verbs: principal English modal verbs are can, could, may, might, must, shall, should, will and would. Certain other verbs are sometimes, but not always, classed as modals; these include ought, had better, and (in certain uses) dare and need.

Modifiers: come either before or after the modified element (the head), depending on the type of modifier and the rules of syntax for the language in question. A modifier placed before the head is called a pre-modifier; one placed after the head is called a post-modifier. For example, in land mines, the word land is a pre-modifier of mines, whereas in the phrase mines in wartime, the phrase in wartime is a post-modifier of mines. A head may have a number of modifiers, and these may include both pre-modifiers and post-modifiers. For example: that nice tall man from Canada whom you met. In this noun phrase, man is the head, nice and tall are pre-modifiers, and from Canada and whom you met are post-modifier. Simple adjectives are usually used as pre-modifiers, with occasional exceptions such as galore (which always appears after the noun) and the phrases time immemorial and court martial (the latter comes from French, where most adjectives are post-modifiers).

Multimodal Texts: many of the texts we read rely on an interaction of written and visual codes. This is especially the case in certain genres such as young children's literature and advertising, where meaning is often dependent on the interplay of writing and images. Texts that rely on more than one code or mode are known as multimodal texts.

Narrator: First-person narration occurs when the narrator of a story is also a participant of the story, signified by the use of the first-person pronoun, I. A first-person narrative may be either autodiegetic, in which the narrator is also the protagonist of the story, or homodiegetic, in which the narrator is a minor character and therefore simply a witness to the experiences of the protagonist. In Daniel Defoe's *Robinson Crusoe*, we find an autodiegetic narrator, as the novel's eponymous hero is also its narrator. In Aphra Behn's *Oroonoko* there is a homodiegetic narrator, as Behn depicts herself as a minor character in the narrative and, therefore, as one privy to its major events: 'I was my self an eye-witness to a great part, of what you will find here set down'. In *Dracula* both autodiegetic and homodiegetic narrators appear.

    A narrator who is not a character in the story but in a way hovers above it and knows everything about it is a heterodiegetic narrator and gives a third person narrative.

Paralinguistic features are to do with body language – laughing whispering.

Phrasal verbs: short phrases whose meanings are different from their constituent lexemes, e.g. 'see to', 'break down, 'put up with', 'wind up'.

Point of view: the way in which events and experiences are filtered through a particular perspective to provide a particular version of reality. Point of view may be: related to how a narrative is presented in terms of space and time through the use of deixis, time frames, and flashbacks and flashforwards; related to a particular ideological viewpoint, such as an individual's way of seeing the world or thinking about events (often in an extreme way). These might be shown through the use of modal verbs, adjectives and adverbs to stress belief or commitment and/or the use of idiosyncratic words and phrases; related to distinguishing between who tells and who sees, as in the case of a narrative told in the third person but which seems to be filtered through a particular character's consciousness.

Pragmatics: the implied meanings of English and how language use creates meanings in interactional contexts; the implied meanings of words, utterances and speech acts in their specific contexts; face, politeness and co-operation in language interaction; how text receivers draw inferences from others' language uses; the influence of different contexts on the meanings of communicative acts; how attitudes, values and ideologies can be signalled through language choices; how language is used to enact and reflect relationships between people.

Prosodic Features These are to do with stress, pitch and tone. These can be conveyed through the use of italics, exclamations and question marks.

Syntax is concerned with sentence structure, function and length. There are three basic sentence functions: Declarative - statement: It was grey; Imperative - command: Get here, right now!; Interrogative - question: Are you okay?

Sentences There are four different sentence types. 1. Minor sentence - this isn't a complete sentence. Look out!' 2. Simple sentence - the simplest complete sentence. Includes a subject, verb and object. 'The cat sat in the rain.' 3. Compound sentence - two or more independent clauses joined by conjunctions (and, but). 'It was raining, but the cat sat there.' 4. Complex sentence - contains at least one subordinate (dependant) clause. 'Because it was raining, the cat moved to sit inside.' ('because it was raining' cannot be understood without the independent clause 'the cat moved to sit inside').

Typographical Features: the features of fonts used in texts such as font type, size and colour (see Graphology).

Vocative: used in addressing or invoking a person or thing. A vocative expression is an expression of direct address where the identity of the party spoken to is set forth expressly within a sentence. For example, in the sentence, 'I don't know, John' John is a vocative expression (with a vocative comma) that indicates the party being addressed. Conversation commonly uses vocatives (address forms) for getting attention and managing interactions. Vocatives often have an attitudinal function in addition to managing the discourse, especially for terms such as honey.

With terms of abuse, whether mild or apparently deeply insulting, we must always remember that they can be turned into covert endearments if said in a particular way in a particular context. However, it is generally true to say that a vocative expression of the type 'you' + adjective + noun is more likely to be unfriendly than friendly, such as 'you dirty bastard', or 'you old cow'.

Further Reading (Fiction and Non-Fiction)

Muriel Barbery, *The Elegance of the Hedgehog*, 2008
T E Carhart, The *Piano Shop on the Left Bank*, 2000
Ernest Hemingway, *On Paris*, 1923
Claude Izner, *Murder on the Eiffel Tower*, 2007
Paula McLain, *The Paris Wife*, 2012
Jeremy Mercer, *Books, Baguettes and Bedbugs*, 2005
Henry Miller, *Tropic of Cancer,* 1934
Patrick Modiano, *Night Watch,* 1971
George Orwell, *Down and Out in Paris and London*, 1933
Hilary Reyl, *Lessons in French*, 2013
Graham Robb, *Parisians*, 2010
Sarah Turnbull, *Almost French*, 2002
Patrick Suskind, *Perfume*, 2010
Edmund White, *The Flaneur*, 2001
Emile Zola, *The Ladies' Delight (Au Bonheur des Dames),* 1883

Visit aqa.org.uk/7707 for the most up-to-date specifications and resources.

Olympia Harbour Publications Inc.

Other Titles in the Critical Study Guide Series include:

Othello in Context – A Critical Study Guide for A Level English E Pushkin, 2020

The Poetry of John Donne – A Critical Study Guide
M Parks, 2016

Dracula – A Critical Study Guide
L Steinmetz, 2016

Frankenstein – A Critical Study Guide
J McLaine, 2015

Thomas Hardy's Poetry – A Critical Study Guide
J McLaine, 2015

Northanger Abbey – A Critical Study Guide
J McLaine, 2013

Tennyson's Poetry – A Critical Study Guide
T Halliwell-Grove, 2012

Olympia Harbour Publications Inc.
Marlinspike Building, Marlinspike Place, Greenwich Conn.

Printed in Great Britain
by Amazon